THEN DARKNESS

S k e t c h e s

Jaydn DeWald (he/they) is the author of *Sheets of Sound* and *The Rosebud Variations*, both from Broken Sleep Books. They are Assistant Professor of English and Director of Creative Writing at Piedmont University in Demorest, Georgia, USA, and serve as managing editor for *COMP: an interdisciplinary journal*.

Also by Jaydn DeWald

BOOKS

The Rosebud Variations	(Broken Sleep Books, 2021)
Sheets of Sound	(Broken Sleep Books, 2020)

PAMPHLETS

common tones in haunted time	(Salò Press, 2023)
7 Miniatures	(Red Bird Chapbooks, 2022)
A Love Supreme: fragments & ephemera	(Quarterly West, 2020)
Out, Voyage	(Broken Sleep Books, 2020)
as counterpoint to this compressed mass a longing	(Sutra Press, 2019)
In Whose Hand the Light Expires	(Yellow Flag Press, 2018)
The Rosebud Variations: And Other Variations	(Greying Ghost Press, 2017)

Each of us has his own rhythm of suffering.
—Roland Barthes

ISBN: 978-1-916938-02-1

The author has asserted their right to be identified as the author of this Work in accordance with the Copyright, Designs and Patents Act 1988

Cover designed by Aaron Kent

Edited and Typeset by Aaron Kent

Broken Sleep Books Ltd
Rhydwen
Talgarreg
Ceredigion
SA44 4HB

Broken Sleep Books Ltd
Fair View
St Georges Road
Cornwall
PL26 7YH

Contents

Self-Portrait with Bari   9

Evening Sketch: After Hopkins   10

5 Evening Sketches: After Jack Gilbert   11

Evening Sketch: After Lou Lipsitz   16

Apprenticeship   17

Vigil with Backyard Pond   19

Evening Sketch: After Eavan Boland   20

Dusk Song   21

Church   22

2 Evening Sketches: After C.D. Wright   23

2 Evening Sketches: After Marvin Bell   25

Evening Sketch: After Calvino   27

Moonless   28

In Bed   29

Notes   31

Acknowledgments   33

Then Darkness
Sketches

Jaydn DeWald

Broken Sleep Books

Self-Portrait with Bari

in rhythm   *i dream he*   is breath-hot   *is fire*

    in hunger   *i leap out*   in neon   is knowing   *the window*

is owl-eyed   *i chase him*   in sweat-glow   *through alleys*

    is shattered   *a smoke trail*   in chordage   *i can't see*   in evening

i call out   in rhythm   *from doorways*   is stagelight   *i listen*   in violence

    he crackles   is owl-eyed   is breath-hot   *i conjure*   in grasping

my bari   is orphaned   *i bellow*   in neon   *he blazes*   in violence

    then quiet   is grasping   *then darkness*   is orphaned   *i touch him*

in chordage   *my lips burn*   in sweat-glow   *become him*

    in stagelight   is shattered   *on all fours*   is hunger

is knowing   *my body*   in evening   *is fire*

Evening Sketch: After Hopkins

i awoke to call   in midwinter in the white
of the morning the moon   in the white of a finger-
nail dwindled and thinned to the fringe
of your photograph   the whites of your eyes
wild looking back askance   held over this candle
your paradisiacal flesh waning but luster-
less under the fruit trees   under dark Maenefa
the mountain i pushed your barrow   your grave dirt up out of the dark
Maenefa the mountain fanged with icicles
and into a moon-   stunned clearing in which lies
our one and only bed   silver-sheeted
its bodies our ghost bodies   dwindled and thinned
in the white of the morning in mid-   copulation entangled
eyelid and eye-   lid i prized open
the desirable sight unsought finally   there you are
held over this candle wild   looking back askance
leaf and leaf divided   from the fringe
of your photo-   graph a page of your flesh
divided   i awoke to call   in flames

5 Evening Sketches: After Jack Gilbert

1.

Darkness for whispers. Sunlight for stones. Roosters for
The village. Clear water for boats. The woman forgotten. Bright heat
For stones. Scent of parsley for nighttime, and fish
For the bones. Radio for ballgames. Her aria forgotten. Rain for still leaves.
Her aria forbidden. For boats a warm breeze. The monk walks for-
ever. Wine for more wine, and whispers forgotten. Rain for ballgames.
Darkness for nighttime. Still leaves for her hair. The bones for
The woman. The village for roosters. Sunlight for boats. Disrobing for
Pleasure, the woman, his ghost. Radio forbidden. For stones a warm breeze.
Clear water for fish. For parsley bright heat. Wine for more wine,
The monk walks alone. Scent of rain for clear water. Her aria for-
ever. Sunlight's for pleasure. Darkness for bones.

2.

breathless through windstorms   masks through
moonlight   the hideouts through fire   red mist through
his sights   throughout the bedrooms   bright cries
through moonlight   blood through ripped sheets, & screaming
through pines   self-   portrait through keyholes
out through their doors   leaves drift through the gutters through-
other their doors   through memories soft-edged O
lovers through-   other   crash through our walls, & ripped
sheets through ladders   drift-leaves through keyholes   breakthrough:
her pines   blood through the ladders her body's   moonlight
fire through bedrooms   masks through his sights   undressing through
mindscapes   hair wild, entwined   self-portrait breakthrough
through storms rides a man   red mist through the
screaming   bright cries through his hands   crash through
our walls   O lovers through hideouts   ripped sheets through
the gutters   leaves drift through   the ladders her
body's self-portrait O breath-   less throughout

3.

flowers in darkness   trout in sunlight   the basement in
ruins   blue clouds in the night   inside the bedroom   bright hair
in sunlight   wrists in silk gloves, and dancing   in lines   black mirrors in
rainstorms   inside the heart   still leaves in the gutters in-   vaded his heart
in the mind a warm breeze   the lovers en-   shrouded   bring in the gods, and silk
gloves in tatters   still leaves in rainstorms   incense in lines   wrists in the gutters
the music inside   ruins in bedrooms   trout in the night   disrobing in
orchards   the woman alight   black mirrors invaded   in storms a man
blue clouds in the dancing   bright hair in his hands   bring in the gods
the lovers in sunlight   still leaves in black mirrors   silk gloves in
the gutters   the music's in tatters it   flowers inside

4.

Ruthless when cornered. Moonlight when cold. Grieving when
Together. Faint music when home. Surrounded when touching. Eyes closed
When cold. Crash of thunder when working, and sleeping
When loved. Crescendoed when horseback. Our shadows when touching. Pain when leaves freeze.
Then darkness: our singing. When home a blank bed. The man drifts when-
ever. Breath when more breath, and touching when cornered. Pain when horseback.
Ruthless when working. Leaves freeze when she cries. Together when
Grieving. Loved when surrounded. Moonlight when home. Electric when
Pressured, surrounded, her ghost. When singing crescendoed. A blank bed when cold.
Faint music when sleeping. When horseback eyes closed. Breath when more breath,
The man drifts alone. Crash of moonlight when cornered. Our shadows when-
ever. Faint thunder when pressured. Then darkness: our love.

5.

pursuer you sculpt me   blue-shadowed in
music   a tritone / my torso   awakened
in darkrooms   is altared electric   distorted all-knowing
dissolving through fingers moon-glittered unending
my navel you   reach in   convulsive throat-clasper
i pull out awakened on   all fours in water
a blues harp emerging   a tritone distorted / red
hair through my organs   you grasp me you reach in
you pull out half-swooning   my navel dissolving ful-
fillment your shoulders my   torso emerging
electric blue shadows then   darkrooms on rockbeds re-
flected a basin   you scoop out unending   drink water
on all fours   pursuer / throat-clasper   moon-
glittered fulfillment you   sculpt me electric
you grasp me your shoulders un-   ending in music

Evening Sketch: After Lou Lipsitz

as shore-mist i take him   as heads bowed as

    sirens   entrance me as terror   as blue sand i lower as

        moonlight dis- / solving his body   is claiming   as candles

    his white lips unlanguaged ascending   i bathe him

as mountains ghost / cloudburst asunder   the earth growls

    the blue notes as gem-   lit as water   i listen at night's edge es-

        caping his body / cold   palms as my witness i   whisper unmoor me

    as mountains he rises as   candles wind-scoured   the earth growls en-

rage me i   bathe him as heads bowed   as white lips at night's edge we

    flash once as lightning   as silent as moonlight / he

        floats out dissolving O   lover as gem-lit wind-   scoured asunder

    as shore-mist unlanguaged   as ghost-clouds i take him

his body's now sirens as- / cending   cold water

Apprenticeship

for decades
  i have knelt

onstage
  pressing

my lips
  to the damp

wood
  over which

a trumpeter
  in smoke &

darkness
  swings

his green
  silk notes

who are you?
  i whisper

how long
  will this last?

he never
  answers

without
  looking down

he drains
  his spit valve

into my open
  mouth

Vigil with Backyard Pond

i guess
i'm too old   to still   see you—
a split-   second, flesh-   colored
blur—   in our leaf-   choked, algae-   clouded   pool:
my hands   are gnarled   & liver-   spotted—
but now,   under-   water,   they look   young again:
once again   your young   mother's hands,
strong enough   to just   snatch you
ashore—

Evening Sketch: After Eavan Boland

echoes where chambers   where voices

join palms   my daughter where kneeling blue

eye-paint where alms   candescence where aching

where snowmelt   is warm   Dublin's night-cold

where burning & absence   where song / un-

photoed where pitch-black   our torchlights where

aching   where drums pound   the whispers our

torchlights where dancing where   arms are deception

a god strikes wher- / ever   cups where more cups: the night holds

my daughter   huddled   where drums pound   our echoes

where burning   *i see you*: an island   my daughter

the kneeling   snowmelt's candescence where

absence is alms / de-   ception where feathers, cicadas,

late Brahms   where huddled un-photoed   a lone bulb where

warm   now absence   affliction & pitch-black

join palms   cups where more cups: a god strikes

alone   Dublin's voices where chambers   blue

torchlights here-   after / our   whispers

my daughter re-   feather your song

Dusk Song

once upon a time   you were not our mother
    framed in the window   we passed at dusk-
light / our green shadow   between us

    an alto sax   projected star-notes / in mid-orbit rose
to meet you   loosely kimonoed through
    mist & cheatgrass / the brass   albatross

cheek to cheek we passed   your arms up-
    lifted under which   the music
surged through us chordless   O veiled conductor / dream

    spellcaster were we not   *your* mothers
darkness absent   in mid-orbit arms &
    no wind / our green shadow   lips like oranges

torn from branches   loosely kimonoed
    projected star-notes / we   framed in the window
dusk-light crescendoed   once upon a time

Church

marble from unions   blue hands from down-   stairs

chalk-dust from rivers-   old   ivory from tears

from dancers'   ascension / black   shoes from downstairs

birds o' standards   from players, & stomping

from prayer   woodwinds from cloakrooms   our solos from dancers

horn from blown hearts / our   solos from players

a cup from blood tears   it's monk time un-

languaged   chords from more chords: the marble   from chambers / from

beechmast from breathwork   two   blown hearts from players

the black shoes from horns / blue   rivers from

standards   prayer from ascension   old hands from down-

stairs   standards from moon-howls   ascension

their tears   black / chalk-dust from woodwinds   a blood cup

from blue   horn   ivory from stomping

from dancers' mud-   rooms   chords from more chords,

it's monk time be-   ware   birds o' downstairs

from stomping   from black shoes   & ivory   blown

solos from un- / ions-   old   marble from tears

2 *Evening Sketches: After C.D. Wright*

1.

the ice   i bruise   his
arms   the swarm   the
mist   i hold   her hair
the floor   i eat   the
cloud   the hands   the dress
i smoke   the eyes, and leave
the head   the lake   the road   her
mouth: the door   i reach   the
moon   we kneel   the form
the page   i sense   the
mist's   the shroud   the
clock   i dream   the bruise
the cloud   i reach   the
lake   the moon: his eyes
the ice   her voice, and wind
her cries   i grasp   the
scent   his arms   her head
the room   the hands   i
eat   the thread   the
ice   the storm   i tear
the dress   re-   fuse the page
his mouth   of thread   the
clock   i dream   we
kneel   the floor   the
wind   the shore   his hands
the storm   i reach   the
room   her hair   the swarm

2.

The bedsheets. The brushwork. The moorlands. The echo. The tritone. The

Rockpool. The closed eye. The cello. The priestess thereafter. The ghost note's

The echo. The thunder, the fingers, and lashing

The tempo. The granite. The stagelight. Her palms out, the power. The black keys. Then inward.

Then darkness: the laughter. The cello. The side glance. A horn wails the-

atrics. The cloudbridge of octaves, and brushwork thereafter. Then inward.

The granite. The bedsheets. The fingers. The black keys. Her moon hair. The tritone's the-

atrics. The rockpool's the cello. The moorlands, the tempo. Illusive, the ghost notes, the priestess de-

shadowed. The closed eye. The counter. The lashing. The echo. Surrender the

Side glance. Her palms out, the tempo. The Octaves of Cloudbridge: a horn wails

The darkness. The laughter. The thunder. The ghost note's the

Counter. Then inward, illusive. The bedsheets. The power.

2 Evening Sketches: After Marvin Bell

1.

Lovers sleeping. Stranger's shudder. Curtains
Rustle. Candles gutter. Mourning silent. Eyelids
Closer. Madness enters. Body's glowing. Vocals
Deeper. Longing's colder. Static rustle. Shadow's fire.
Breathless shudder. Music mourning. Heartbeats' gasp-
ing. Shadow's alley. Lovers enter. Bodies colder.
Verdant raining. Stranger's meadow. Mourning's
Shudder. Curtains tattered. Vocals' fire. Static
Photo. Eyelids colder. Heartbeats' echo. Body's
Gutter. Silent also. Candles sleeping. Madness closer.
Longing deeper. Music's fire. Breathless gasp-
ing. Stranger's echo. Raining fire. Lovers' glow.

2.

Cosmic heart-rooms. Haloed center. Fretboards'
Organs. Lamplight's fingers. Searing tenors. Whispered
Vapor. Ghosting bodies. Gold-flecked stages. Faces
Colder. Rain-pocked solo. Fingers lonesome. Sequins swallowed.
Patterns abstract. Cello's center. Black keys swing-
ing. Late-night walking. Lonesome wander. Snow's erasure.
Song embodied. Sequined minor. Searing
Organs. Lamplight spidered. Gold-flecked shoulders. Rain-pocked
Tenor. Lyric patterns. Black keys swallowed. Whispered
Colder. Body's cello. Fingers' heart-rooms. Fretboards haloed.
Fading minor. Hair's erasure. Moonrise swing-
ing. Late-night solo. Walking vapor. Cosmic ghost.

Evening Sketch: After Calvino

what story down there   outside the town of Malbork
     illuminated on the carpet of leaves what   story down there
by the moon   in a network of lines that in-   tersect my son
     a traveler in the gathering shadow   leaning in a network
from the steep slope of lines that enlace   in a network what
     by the moon looks down there down   in the wigs of grass

around an empty grave of wind or vertigo if   on a winter's
     night a traveler my son   on the blue swirling carpet outside
the town of Malbork leaning   with young arms up-
     raised by the moon around an empty grave what   story down
there awaits in the shadow gathering   its end my one son
     on the carpet of leaves that inter-   sect looks down there

from the steep slope   of wind or vertigo at me without   fear
     what awaits gathering without fear   illuminated its end?

Moonless

the spirits   *i follow*   need singing   *a lantern*

      need echoes   *through static*   pine forests   my brother   *a table*

unbodied   *she rises*   in ribbons   *from water*

      meet darkness   *i cower*   our cabin   *she enters*   reflected

in synth-green   the spirits   *i whisper*   feed hunger   *in tritones*   he listens

      the calling   unbodied   needs singing   *from cellars*   desire

i lure in   my oboe   *she answers*   pine forests   *electric*   he listens

      then quiet   desire   *in grave mist*   our cabin   *awakened*

the spirits   *she exhales*   in ribbons   *i swallow*

      feed hunger   need echoes   *i walk out*   meet darkness

my brother   *a lantern*   reflected   *i follow*

In Bed

he cannot
  not pretend
the late-night

winter wind
  is her slum-
brous breathing

beside him
  in the empty
dark again

Notes

The Barthes epigraph is from his *Mourning Diary*, trans. Richard Howard.

Page 10: "Evening Sketch: After Hopkins" borrows language from Gerard Manley Hopkins' "Moonrise."

Page 11: "5 Evening Sketches: After Jack Gilbert" was inspired by Gilbert's "The Forgotten Dialect of the Heart."

Page 16: "Evening Sketch: After Lou Lipsitz" was inspired by Lipsitz's "Cold Water."

Page 20: "Evening Sketch: After Eavan Boland" was inspired by Boland's "The Lost Land."

Page 23: "2 Evening Sketches: After C.D. Wright" derives its form from Wright's "Flame."

Page 25: "2 Evening Sketches: After Marvin Bell" derives its form from Bell's "Spot Six Differences."

Page 27: "Evening Sketch: After Calvino" borrows language from the titles of the fragmented fictions in Italo Calvino's *If on a winter's night a traveler.*

Acknowledgments

Props to the editors of the following publications in which versions of these poems first appeared: *The Adroit Journal, Bat City Review, Bath Magg, Blue Earth Review, Brilliant Corners: A Journal of Jazz & Literature, Cape Magazine, december, Diagram, Fourteen Hills, Nashville Review, The North, The Offing, Poet Lore, Spoon River Poetry Review, Stonecoast Review, Witness,* and *The Woodward Review.*

"Apprenticeship" was published in *Masculinity: An Anthology of Modern Voices,* ed. Rick Dove, Aaron Kent, and Stuart McPherson (Broken Sleep Books, 2024).

PLAY OUT YOUR UNREST

www.ingramcontent.com/pod-product-compliance
Lightning Source LLC
Chambersburg PA
CBHW021946040426
42448CB00008B/1270